A Feast of Graces

101 rhyming graces for group meals

by Douglas Aitken

Scottish
Christian PRESS

First published in Great Britain
in 2003 by Scottish Christian Press
21 Young Street
Edinburgh EH2 4HU

ISBN 1904325149

Cover illustration by Nial Smith
Illustrations by Sharon Scotland
Book layout by Heather Macpherson

Printed and bound in the UK by Datacolor Imaging

Printed in 2003. Reprinted in 2004.

Dedication

For Fiona - whose patience is infinite (so far),
and for my colleagues of Alloa Rotary Club.

About the author

Douglas Aitken took retirement as a Church of Scotland minister after having served as a minister in Nairobi and also Clackmannan, and worked in the Religious Department of BBC Scotland for eighteen years. Now he's "retired", he's currently assisting several local churches in Stirling, producing religious programmes for Central FM local radio, and writing a weekly column in the Wee County News. A Past president of Alloa Rotary Club, he is webmaster of the club's website and convener of the Kirk's Internet forum.

Douglas Aitken's preaching, writing and broadcasting show that he has a 'way with words' which he uses to share his faith. These rhyming graces are a fun way of doing just that.

Contents

Introduction

It all began by my being called upon, without warning, to say grace for the weekly lunch of the Alloa Rotary Club. I used a grace told me by a former Moderator of the General Assembly of the Church of Scotland. The Very Rev Dr Bill Johnston had been called upon by the Archbishop of Canterbury to say grace for a meeting of the British Council of Churches, as it was called then, and had responded by addressing the Almighty on behalf of this august body with the words:

'Lord, bless this bunch
as they munch their lunch.
Amen.'

This appealed to my sense of humour. I have always believed that grace is the proper way to start a meal - but I despair of those who transform the giving of simple thanks into a solemn sermon or some tedious instruction to the Almighty. To do it in verse or rhyme just adds to the fun. I would have to say, however, that the need to provide a new one each time I am invited to say grace does tax my ingenuity. There are, after all, a very limited number of rhymes for such occasions. Anyway, to those who care to use them or adapt them for their own use - you do so with my blessing. All these graces have been used at meetings of Alloa Rotary Club, which explains the emphasis on lunch and the references to Presidents and other Rotary things! However, they are all adaptable for more general use, and we have offered some suggestions to help with this (options to the suggested word are usually indicated by an oblique line - such as 'business/issues'). But if none of the choices suggested applies, or you have a specific change which suits your occasion, feel free to make it. Moreover, a particular grace may stimulate an alternative rhyme of your own. That, too, means the book has served its purpose.

Whatever your reasons for reading the book, I hope you find it helpful and fun.

Douglas Aitken

Foregrace:

a few words before tucking in...

Lord, I often think and pray -
I cannot face another day
when once more I must compose
a grace in rhyme instead of prose.
Yet from the web and various places
the cheques come in for books of graces.
So may our thankfulness be blessed
with food and cash and all the rest.
Amen

For what we are about to receive…

1

Lord at such a time as this,
facing gastronomic bliss,
our tendency to dive right in
might well be counted mortal sin.
So help us pause before the fare,
to offer you this thankful prayer.
Amen

2

Lord we pray your gracious blessing
on the matter that's most pressing -
experiential gastronomics,
silencing our loudest comics -
for which we offer thanks as good
as those we offer for the food.
Amen

3

Lord we give you thankful praise
for everything the menu says;
and though there isn't toast to crunch,
just bless us as we munch our lunch.
Amen

4

Lord bless this gastronomic force
and our loquacious intercourse.
And save us Lord, at my suggestion,
from both kinds of indigestion.
Amen

5

Where e'er our conversations roam,
with talk of work and sport and home,
accept our thanks that upward rise
like smoking incense to the skies.
Then guard us Lord, as pure within,
we turn to gastronomic sin
Amen

6

Lord we voice our appreciation
for our coming culinary sensation,
and offer you our invitation
to bless our lunchtime conversation.
Amen

7

Lord, for food
that's good
our praise
we raise.
Amen

8

We thank you, Lord,
for this repast,
at last.
Amen

9

Dear Lord,
a word
of praise
we raise
for food
that's good
and time
to rhyme.
until we're full,
that's cool.
Amen

In grateful thanks

10

Lord, as we take our lunchtime places
with those our fellowship embraces.
Sitting here with smiling faces,
in serried ranks.
We offer you the simplest graces:
our humble thanks.
Amen

11

Lord, we bow before you now
in thankful mood for coming food;
and may your touch, which matters much,
bless us again we pray,
Amen.

12

Lord, as we take our chosen place,
we offer first our simple grace:
accept our thanks for food to eat
and bless the people that we meet.
Amen

13

Lord, here we are, this thankful crew
with ample meat and sweet to chew,
while conversations we renew
until we're full.
Yet all this goodness comes from you -
dear Lord - that's cool!
Amen

14

Lord, as we each sit in our place,
we offer you this simple grace:
may our fellowship be good
accept our thankfulness for food
and as we meet with friends and brothers
remind us of the needs of others.
Amen

15

O God, who set the stars in place
and gave the sun to warm our face,
accept from us this thankful grace:
for food and friends,
and for this respite from the race
that never ends.
Amen

16

Lord, as we sit for our lunchtime / evening meal
accept the thankfulness we feel
shining from expectant faces
sitting in our chosen places.
So bless the food which we partake
and bless us all for Jesus' sake.
Amen

17

Lord we live,
and all believe,
that as we give
we shall receive.
Accept our thanks
we offer now,
as in our ranks
our heads we bow,
then bless our food
that it may raise
our doing good
throughout our days.
Amen

Seasonal; and special days

18

Lord, we thank you
for food to eat,
and friends to greet,
and willing feet
for service to bring,
and signs of spring -
and everything.
Amen

19

Lord, we bring our thankful praise
for food and friends and sunny days.
Be present as we meet together
and share our joy of brilliant weather.
But for the farmers, to ask is right
a little rain - but through the night.
Amen

20

Lord
After weeks with the weather dry
you have heard the farmers' cry,
and sent some ground-refreshing rain
which makes the rest of us complain.
But no meteorological phrase
can dim the prayer of thankful praise
for your most gracious gift of food,
and for the power for doing good.
So let our meeting here be blessed
and our fellowship the very best.
Amen

21

Lord we offer thanks and praise
for sun and warmth these past few days;
and, though the clouds may gather, still
our jackets we discard at will,
and praise you more for food for eating,
and ask your blessing on our meeting.
Amen

22

The sun is shining, to our relief,
it cheers our day beyond belief.
So as we meet for fish or beef
we offer you this thankful prayer:
to bless to us the food we share
and fellowship, none can compare,
for after we have finished eating,
we're stuck with another business / monthly /
blessed (!) meeting

Autumn / Winter

23

Lord, with thankfulness we pray
it hasn't really rained today.
At least, not yet / much, and everyone
has caught a fleeting glimpse of sun.
We come to you in thankful mood
for our choice of coming food.
Amen

24

We bow our heads before you, Lord,
in thankfulness with one accord
for the food that we have chosen
and, while outside the ground is frozen,
we are sheltered safe from harm,
our fellowship to keep us warm.
Amen

25

Lord, I thank you that I'm free
to sit among this company
and meet with visitors and friends
in the fellowship, which never ends.
So bless our gathering today,
and hear the thankfulness we pray.
And bless our guests both young and old,
and bring us warmth instead of cold.
Amen

Come rain or shine...

26

Lord, as a group we come together
to talk of issues / interests / business and the weather,
to share our worries and our fun
expressing pleasure for the sun / though sad we
cannot see the sun!
and now we all are feeling good,
we give you thanks for coming food.
Amen

27

Lord, we cope whate'er the weather sends
as long as we can meet with friends,
and we will serve the world enough,
no matter if the going's tough.
For that's the purpose of our guild,
to see our hopes and plans fulfilled.
So thank you for this lunchtime / evening food,
and bless our thoughts of doing good.
Amen

28

Lord, as we stand around and blether
we talk of changes in the weather;
but as we sit to eat our fill
we ask your blessing unchanging still.
May our food and fellowship be fine
and our will to serve, divine.
Amen

Christmas

29

Lord, let your blessing be on this bunch,
as we sit down to Christmas lunch.
May our fellowship and food
keep us serving as we should.
Listen to our Christmas song
saving us from every wrong.
Guard each one of us from greed
reminding us of those in need.
Amen

30

Lord, bless the food we munch for lunch
and make us all a merry bunch,
that we can make, like Christmas elves,
our service come before ourselves.
Amen

New Year

31

Lord, before us now the table's set,
accept our thanks for what we get
and may our fellowship and cheer
hang over in the coming year...
Amen

32

Lord, once more we come to take our place
and offer you our grateful grace:
for food and friends and festive cheer
and ask your blessing on this year.
Amen

Lent

33

Lord, we thank you for this coming repast
a week before the Lenten fast
and for all good things which we concede
are calculated to meet our need.
And as we come to masticate,
teach us, too, to circulate.
Amen

Weekdays

34

Lord, as I journeyed to this place,
I penned a rhyme, just in case
our president / meeting leader called for a grace.
So hear our thanks, Lord, and our praise
offered up on <u>Wednes</u>/days,
for goodness that can still amaze,
for meat
and sweet
and friends to greet,
hills to climb,
and words to rhyme -
I'm out of time -
dear Lord again.
Amen

Dinners and dances

35

Lord I stand 'mong hungry sinners
to ask your blessing on their dinners,
with starters, main course, then a sweet,
may all our feasting be complete,
and leave us with the strength perchance
to venture on the floor to dance.
And may the raffle's / tombola's great proceeds
help to serve some people's needs.
So after this extended grace,
let fun and laughter fill this place.
Amen

36

Lord, before you we advance
and ask with humble upward glance,
for blessings from you to enhance
our festive verve;
that as we eat and talk and dance,
we also serve.
Amen

Fellowship and goodwill

37

Lord, as we gather for our meeting,
bless to us the food we're eating.
Accept our thanks and grateful praise.
Enrich our fellowship all our days.
Amen.

38

Lord, we ask your gracious blessing
as, to see our work progressing
and feel our fellowship refreshing,
we fill this place.
Now our thankfulness expressing,
Lord, hear our grace.
Amen

39

Lord, hear us as we bow in prayer
with thanks for the fellowship we share
and food to eat and work to do.
May it bring glory unto you.
Amen

40

Lord, as we take our chosen chairs,
we offer you our simple prayers,
our grateful thanks for food to eat
and fellowship with friends we meet.
Amen

41

Lord, before we start our lunchtime / evening fare,
we offer up this simple prayer:
we thank you for the food we eat,
and for the fellowship we meet.
Amen

42

I am here, Lord, another time,
looking for a grace in rhyme.
A social time is why we meet,
so bless the food we're going to eat,
and bless the fellowship before and after
and fill our lives with pleasant laughter.
Amen

43

Lord we come from life's great race
knowing that we have to face
another wretched rhyming grace.
This noble bunch!
So send your blessing on this place
and on our lunch.
Amen

44

When I came to lunch today
I didn't have a grace to say.
But pen and paper put that right
and now I pray with all my might:
our thanks for fellowship and food,
and ask our work for you / business here be good.
Amen

45

We thank you Lord for lunchtime / evening fare
and for the fellowship we share,
and ask that you will hear this prayer
(although it's one I kept for spare).
Amen

46

Lord, in my pocket, just in case,
I keep an extra lunchtime/dinner grace,
to ask your blessing on this place
and on our meal.
And may our fellowship have space
for added zeal.
Amen

47

Lord, we bow in earnest prayer,
to thank you for our lunchtime/evening fare
and for the fellowship we share,
with which few others can compare,
because it gives us strength to dare
to give the time we have to spare,
and even more, to serve and care.
With our President / leader in the chair
and the rest of us assembled where
we found a friend and an empty chair.
Amen

Absent-minded graces

After an absence

48
Lord, at last I'm back to take my place
and offer you a rhyming grace,
to give you grateful thanks and praise
for your providence all our days.
So bless our food, and as we feed,
keep us mindful of those in need.
Amen

Filling in

49
Lord,
Someone else was saying grace
but they've been called to a different place.
So I am left among these ranks
to offer you our grateful thanks:
for food and fellowship at lunch
and words to stimulate this bunch.
Amen

50
Lord, we thought today
that someone else would pray,
but now I fear, s/he is not here,
so in her/his place, I give this grace:
just bless the food
that's good.
Amen

When others have filled in

51

Lord, we come again today,
knowing that we have to pray
our thanks to you for every good,
for fellowship and coming food;
so bless us in our chosen places,
with thanks to others for saying graces.
Amen

For latecomers

52

As grace is spoken while we wait
for sustenance to fill our plate
more than enough,
if none is left for those who're late
then, Lord, that's tough!
Amen

53

Here we are Lord, right on time,
with yet another grace in rhyme,
to give thanksgiving, as we should,
for fellowship and coming food.
We're back to soup and meat or fish.
What more could any person wish?
Except perhaps a smaller plate
for anyone who comes in late.
Amen

For naming and shaming a notorious late-comer..!

54

Lord, we think your providence is great,
accept the words of thanks we state:
for food that's served upon our plate,
and hasten on the day and date
that _____ _____ isn't late!
Amen

For non-attenders...

55

Hear our thanks, Lord, as we pray,
meeting at the close / this time of day,
send your blessing on this place
in answer to this rhyming grace,
and your righteous judgement send
on those who simply won't attend.
But may it be your gracious will
our friendship cup of love to fill.
Amen

Meeting eating

General

56
Lord, we've come with friendly greeting,
and chosen each our table seating.
Accept our thanks for what we're eating,
and bless us in our business / this time of meeting.
Amen

57
Lord, it's my turn once again
to give a grace from my rhyming pen.
To thank you for our food and then
to bless our eating,
and seek your godly guidance when
we start our meeting.
Amen

58
Lord, we gather in our chosen seating
and come to constitute our meeting,
asking blessing on our eating,
sincerity in every greeting,
and service that is never fleeting,
in everything your love repeating
and in your name.
Amen

59
Lord, we thank you for your care,
reflected in the meal we share
because if business is too deep,
with good excuses, we can sleep.
Amen

60

Lord, there always comes a time
to have a grace without a rhyme,
but as that time is not today,
accept our thanks for food, we pray,
and when we all have finished eating,
let your Spirit bless our meeting.
Amen

61

Lord, accept this grateful grace
for all your blessings on this place,
and for your providence we trace
in food for eating.
So may your goodness still embrace
our lunchtime / evening meeting.
Amen

62

Lord, belief in existential grace,
your omnipresence in this place,
and full forgiveness for transgressions,
leads us to make our full confessions.
So let our lives be sanctified
and this our meeting justified.
Amen

Speedy business

63

Lord, a wave of thanks comes from this room
for all the food that we'll consume,
and a prayer, Lord, we confess,
that you'll expedite the business.
Amen

64

Lord, you know it is a pain -
I have to offer grace again
when I have hardly had the time
to think of something that will rhyme.
So from these expectant ranks,
I offer you our grateful thanks
and pray that after what we eat,
the business may be short and sweet.
Amen

65

Lord, as we take our chosen seat,
we give you thanks for food to eat
and praise you for the friends we meet
- their service strong -
and hope the business on the sheet
is not too long.
Amen

66

We thank you, Lord, for our two courses,
invigorating tired resources.
When coffee comes and business starts,
help us to work with willing hearts.
Amen

For the Chair / President / Speaker

67

Lord, as we gather safe and sound,
in respite from the daily round,
we thank you for the bill of fare
and our president / leader in the chair.
May our fellowship be the light
that makes our service / hard work good and right.
Amen

68

We come now, Lord, to ask you fair
to bless our president / leader in the chair
and to give you thanks, this happy bunch,
for the food we chose for lunch;
for friends to meet and goals to chase;
and rolls consumed before the grace.
Amen

Lord, we gather in congregation,
engaged in active conversation,
hoping that we might be fed
with something more than daily bread.
For those who've started on their roll
your judgement bell shall surely toll,
but bless the rest of us for being good
and bless to us the *coming* food;
and just to make things right and fair,
bless the chairman / leader in their chair.
Amen

70

Lord, as we gather for our meeting
it falls to me to grace our eating.
For the food we praise your name,
and ask your blessing just the same
on our friendly conversation
and our speaker's presentation,
and energise our service / business part
for which we pray with humble heart.
Amen

71

Lord, we offer this thankful grace
for food and friendship in this place,
and, though we eat not lunch but dinner,
look kindly on each hungry sinner.
Then when we all have finished eating
bless the speaker / leader at our meeting.
Amen

Club, Society, or other business

(This section has some graces particularly appropriate to regular
business meetings such as those of the Rotary Clubs; but can be
adapted to any other regular meetings with a little adjusting.)

72

Lord, business looms again once more
which some may think a weekly / monthly / yearly bore.
When treasurers describe the coffers
and club convenors / organisers make their offers
of work to do and service good.
Thank heaven it all begins with food!
Amen

73

Lord, receive our thankful grace
for all your blessings on this place:
for food and friendships firm and true
and more club / of our business still to do.
Amen

74

Lord, our business / annual / current meeting means
debate
on things like fines for being late,
or eating rolls before the grace,
and other crimes done in this place:
divesting jackets un-permitted -
such things by which our teeth are gritted.
So ere such conflict is our mood,
Accept our grateful thanks for food.
Amen

75

We pause, good Lord, before we eat
to give you thanks for soup and meat.
Then bless the business we conclude
to run the club / this group the way we should.
Forgive the errors we may make
and keep us true for your name's sake.
Amen

Here we are, Lord, us and them
gathered for our AGM.
Electing officers for future years
by acclamation and with cheers
but first, good Lord, we have our eats,
sandwiches with different meats,
for which we give you thanks and praise,
even on the dullest days.
But then, dear Lord, don't think us wrong,
we pray the business may not be long.
Amen

Service to others

77

Help us Lord, so good and kind,
to keep our youth in heart and mind,
leaving lethargy behind,
by doing good;
and then, if you are so inclined,
just bless our food.
Amen

78

Lord, as we sit here face to face,
be pleased to hear our thankful grace;
for food prepared for our delight
and conversation that's just right,
to help us do the service / useful part,
fleet of foot and light of heart.
Amen

79

Lord, bless our business and our food,
and help us serve the way we should,
That all our members make a team
to let us follow our service dream.
Amen

80

Lord, as we sit down to our lunch,
with thanks for Melba toast to crunch
and soup to sup and meat to munch,
we ask your blessing on this bunch.
Make our friendship more than a hunch
and may our service / helping pack some punch.
Amen

81

Lord, you are our unseen guest.
Accept the thanks herewith expressed
by hungry people on a quest:
for food and fellowship of the best.
So may you send your peaceful dove
to bring your blessings from above,
and give our energies a shove
to help us serve the world with love.
Amen

82

Lord, we thank you for our food
and our fellowship with friends.
Keep us faithful in doing good,
ensure our service never ends.
Amen

83

Lord, bless the people in this room
and bless the food that we consume.
Be in our talk, our service share.
Accept our thanks and hear our prayer.
Amen

84

Lord, please hear us when we pray
our grateful thanks for food today
and for the gift of faithful friends
and service / hard work on which the world depends.
Amen

85

Lord, we ask your blessing on our group,
as we start with juice or soup,
bless our friendship as we eat
our share of salad or of meat.
May our fellowship give us nerve
properly the world to serve.
Amen

86

We thank you, Lord, for all things good:
for fellowship and ample food,
for service done and still to do,
accept the grace we offer you.
Amen

87

I stand in this exalted place
and offer you a simple grace:
we thank you, Lord, for food to eat,
for service planned and friends to greet,
and people to congratulate -
so help us now to celebrate.
Amen

88

We thank you, Lord,
for food prepared,
for friendship shared,
for service dared;
and ask you, Lord,
to bless them all.
Amen

89

Here we are, Lord, gathered friends,
on which our very life depends,
met to laugh and chat and burn
to be the ones to whom we turn
when all life's planning falls apart
and there to find a helpful heart.
So bless our fellowship and food
and bless our laughter and our mood,
and may our meeting energise
our work, should any need arise.
Amen

The World

Peace

90

Lord, hear us as we take our places,
expectation on our faces,
thanking you with rhyming graces
for food and chat and this oasis,
which gives, amid life's stressful races,
peace.
Amen

91

Lord, bless our fellowship we pray,
accept our thanks for food today,
and keep us mindful as we feed
of those in danger and in need;
and may our meeting here increase
our will to live and work for peace
Amen

92

Lord, hear our praise,
that all our days
your goodness sends
our food and friends.
So as we meet
to talk and eat,
help us to heed
the folk in need
and hear their cry;
our service try
your good to share.
Give everywhere
a blessing then -
true peace.
Amen

Those in Need

93

Lord, hear thanksgiving from this room
for the food that we'll consume.
But as we tackle fish or meat,
and highly calorific sweet,
keep us mindful as we feed
of hungry souls in greater need.
Amen

94

Remember, Lord, this merry bunch
in conversation over lunch.
In thankfulness your grace requesting
for the food that we're digesting,
and asking that our service / efforts speed
some greater good for those in need.
Amen

95

Lord, we thank you for this meal
and for the fellowship we feel.
Help us to make our service / hard work real
for those in need;
that, answering your call to heal
we sow a seed.
Amen

96

Lord, your gracious goodness sends
abundant food and faithful friends.
So hear the thankfulness we raise
in honest prayer and grateful praise,
and may our fellowship precede
our greater work for those in need.
Amen

97

Lord, again it's time to pray
in thankfulness for food today,
and for your blessings, which are many,
though some there are who don't have any.
So may our fellowship and fun
bring greater good to everyone.
Amen

98

Lord, as we sit here face to face
we offer thanksgiving in our grace
for your provision of all things good,
and ask your blessing on our food.
Remembering your bounties many,
we think of those who don't have any.
In Jesus' name,
Amen

99

Lord, hear us as in earnest prayer
we thank you for our bill of fare;
teach us always how to care
for those in need;
and may our service ever dare
good to exceed.
Amen

100

Lord, as we meet for this dinner,
with not a chance of growing thinner,
we pray that every hungry sinner
may thankful be,
and this whole evening be a winner
for charity.
Amen

Aftergrace:

be thankful for small mercies...

Lord, we pray you not to glower,
but smile upon our business hour.
That as in fellowship we feed,
our thoughts may reach to those in need.
Last week another gave a grace
'twas offered in a different place
of sixteen lines, words in a spate.
You'll be glad to know mine's only eight.
Amen